WORD PLAY!
WRITE YOUR OWN
CRAZY COMICS
#1

CHUCK WHELON

DOVER PUBLICATIONS, INC.
MINEOLA, NEW YORK

NOTE

Use your imagination to fill the speech balloons in this delightful book with your own clever dialogue. Look at the panels for each comic and get the story line, and then come up with the words. You'll find scenes at a baseball game, a carnival, and in a jungle, and you'll encounter a dragon, a frog princess, a mummy, a UFO, and even Frankenstein. Enjoy creating your own comics with these memorable characters and settings—and many more!

Bibliographical Note

Word Play! Write Your Own Crazy Comics #1 is a new work, first published by Dover Publications, Inc., in 2011.

International Standard Book Number

ISBN-13: 978-0-486-48165-4
ISBN-10: 0-486-48165-4

Manufactured in the United States by RR Donnelley
48165404   2015
www.doverpublications.com

ART MUSEUM

1

BABYSITTER

BAKING

BASEBALL

BASKETBALL

BBQ

BIG FOOT

BIRTHDAY GIRL

BOWLING

CAFETERIA

CAMEL RACE

CAR

CARNIVAL PRIZE

CARNIVAL RIDE

CLOWNS

COMPUTER

CURFEW

DESERT

DINER

DOG WALK

DRAGON

EAGLE

FIREFLIES

FRANKENSTEIN

GIFT

HOMEWORK

HORSE

JUNGLE

ICE CREAM

MOON

MOVIE THEATER

35

NESSIE

MUMMY

MUSIC ROOM

PARTY DRESS

PHOTOGRAPHER

PIRATES

43

PLANE

PLAY

POLE VAULT

POOL SHARK

SKATEBOARD

SANDCASTLE

SCARY MOVIE

SKIING

SNACK

SNORKELERS

STRONGMAN

SUPERMARKET

SURFERS

UFO

UMBRELLA

WEREWOLF

WRONG DOOR

"XTRA" SCARY STORY